Teaching Pronunciation

John Murphy

English
Language
Teacher
Development
Series

Thomas S. C. Farrell,
Series Editor

Typeset in Janson and Frutiger
by Capitol Communications, LLC, Crofton, Maryland USA
and printed by Gasch Printing, LLC, Odenton, Maryland USA

TESOL International Association
1925 Ballenger Avenue
Alexandria, Virginia 22314 USA
Tel 703-836-0774 • Fax 703-836-7864

Publishing Manager: Carol Edwards
Cover Design: Tomiko Breland
Copyeditor: Sarah J. Duffy

TESOL Book Publications Committee
John I. Liontas, Chair

Maureen S. Andrade   Joe McVeigh
Jennifer Lebedev   Gail Schafers
Robyn L. Brinks Lockwood   Lynn Zimmerman

Project overview: John I. Liontas and Robyn L. Brinks Lockwood
Reviewer: Aubrey Bronson

Copyright © 2013 by TESOL International Association

All rights reserved. Copying or further publication of the contents of this work are
not permitted without permission of TESOL International Association, except for
limited "fair use" for educational, scholarly, and similar purposes as authorized by
U.S. Copyright Law, in which case appropriate notice of the source of the work
should be given.

Every effort has been made to contact the copyright holders for permission to re-
print borrowed material. We regret any oversights that may have occurred and will
rectify them in future printings of this work.

ISBN 9781931185103

Contents

About the Author

John M. Murphy is Professor of Applied Linguistics at Georgia State University, USA. His professional interests include second language teacher development, teaching the spoken language, and reflective teaching practices. He is co-editor of *Understanding the Courses We Teach: Local Perspectives on English Language Teaching* (University of Michigan Press, 2001). John is also a yoga instructor in the lineage of Pranakriya Hatha Yoga.

Series Editor's Preface

The English Language Teacher Development (ELTD) Series consists of a set of short resource books for English language teachers that are written in a jargon-free and accessible manner for all types of teachers of English (native and nonnative speakers of English, experienced and novice teachers). The ELTD Series is designed to offer teachers a theory-to-practice approach to English language teaching, and each book offers a wide variety of practical teaching approaches and methods for the topic at hand. Each book also offers opportunities for teachers to interact with the materials presented. The books can be used in preservice settings or in-service courses and can also be used by individuals looking for ways to refresh their practice.

John Murphy's book *Teaching Pronunciation* explores different approaches to teaching pronunciation in the second language classroom. Murphy provides a comprehensive overview of pronunciation with a focus on thought groups and prominence and the teaching of pronunciation in an easy-to-follow guide that language teachers will find very practical for their own contexts. Topics covered include concepts of pronunciation; teaching and learning pronunciation; syllables and individual words; and vowels, consonants, and body language. *Teaching Pronunciation* is a valuable addition to the literature in our profession.

I am very grateful to the authors who contributed to the ELTD Series for sharing their knowledge and expertise with other TESOL professionals because they have done so willingly and without any compensation to make these short books affordable to language teachers throughout the world. It was truly an honor for me to work with each of these authors as they selflessly gave up their valuable time for the advancement of TESOL.

Thomas S. C. Farrell

1

Concepts to Support
Teaching and Learning

To set the stage for a discussion of pronunciation teaching, look at an excerpt adapted from a local television news report. In it, a female airline passenger is being interviewed about an emergency at the end of her flight from Los Angeles to Miami. After introducing the woman as a "hero," the reporter asked her to describe her experiences on the plane. Please note that the transcript is punctuation-free.

The Airplane Aisle Incident

". . . the plane landed the cabin lights turned on everyone got out of their seats I stepped into the aisle opened the overhead compartment and was waiting my turn to leave the plane in back of me I heard a noise that didn't sound right when I turned I saw an older man was falling into a woman behind him he looked scared his face was stone white I didn't think he was breathing I yelled for help and then a couple of us moved into action the first thing I did was to get the people behind me to back away by this point most of the aisle had cleared so we were able to stretch him out on the floor I heard someone say we have to get him out of the plane so I grabbed his legs this tall guy grabbed his shoulders and we carried him off I know CPR so I cleared a space made sure everyone else was out of the way . . . fortunately when it was all over he fully recovered seemed to be fine . . ."

Thought Groups and Pausing

Taking a closer look at the first few lines shows that Excerpt 1 is divided into short segments based on the speaker's actual delivery:

The Airplane Aisle Incident: Excerpt 1

the plane landed // the cabin lights turned on // everyone got out of their seats // I stepped into the aisle // opened the overhead compartment // and was waiting my turn to leave the plane

---

The double slash marks indicate one of several rhythmic features that can serve as momentary boundaries between clusters of words in spoken English. These may be a full break in the stream of speech, a lengthening, or a holding of the word at the end of a word cluster before the next cluster begins. Two examples of words that would be lengthened or held longer in this way are underlined below:

// the cabin lights turned **on** // everyone got out of their **seats** //

Lane (2010) explains that in cases of a lengthening or holding of syllables, these "may be heard as a pause, although within an utterance, the voice 'lingers' rather than stops" at the boundary of a word cluster (p. 52). For ease of presentation, I refer to such boundary markers as *pauses,* and to the clusters of words between them as *thought groups.* Following these conventions, the double slash marks featured in Excerpt 1 indicate five pauses and six thought groups for what otherwise might have been an uninterrupted stream of speech. As the passenger was telling her story, her pauses were very brief, many barely noticeable, and most provided insufficient time for even a very quick intake of breath. Such pauses are a completely normal feature of spoken English that make possible its characteristic rhythmic nature (Brazil, 1994). Pauses reflect momentary breaks in the flow of speech tied to the speaker's communicative intent as well as both the speaker's and listener's needs for message organization. Though written texts in English provide clear divisions between words to simplify the process of reading, spoken language simply does not work that way. Rather, we speak in thought groups within which clusters of words are tightly strung together, forming intermittent pulses of speech (Lane, 2010).

REFLECTIVE BREAK

- From the discussion so far, why was the Airplane Aisle
  Incident narrative initially presented punctuation-free?

- What might be some implications for preparing teaching
  materials?

Introducing Thought Groups

One way to introduce the concept of thought grouping is to present
learners with examples of identical prepositions that sometimes occur
together. More technically, these identical words usually involve the
second element of a two-word verb followed immediately by the same
word functioning as a preposition. Such dual occurrences of the same
words right next to each other can serve as powerful illustrations of the
need for speakers to insert pauses at meaningful locations while speaking. Here are some examples:

- Why don't you think it over // over the weekend?
- What time does the doctor come in // in the afternoon?
- Who can we turn to // to learn more?
- This is exactly what I've been waiting for // for years.

Though this book also covers other facets of pronunciation, if the
time you have available to teach pronunciation is limited, by all means
prioritize the process of thought grouping. Or if you have sufficient
time to attend to other facets of English pronunciation, be sure to
teach the process of thought grouping early on and continue spiraling
back to it. An awareness of how thought groups operate is essential for
clearer understanding of most components of English pronunciation
that are teachable in English as a second or foreign language (ESL/
EFL) classrooms (Brazil, 1994; Dickerson, 2010). All such components
are anchored within the thought group. Some priorities when teaching
pronunciation are to build learner awareness of what thought groups
are, to define them in relation to the pauses that both surround and
help delineate them, and to teach thought groups directly in ESL and
EFL classrooms.

Why Are Thought Groups Helpful?

A compelling reason to teach the process of thought grouping is that it provides needed time for speakers to organize their thoughts. Another reason is that when a speaker's message is well organized and presented in meaningful units, listeners have an easier time comprehending it. "The brief pauses or holding at the end of a thought group slows the student down, giving him or her more time to make [appropriate] lexical, grammatical, and pronunciation choices" (Lane, 2010, p. 53). Here is a list of pronunciation features that may be taught more efficiently once learners are familiar with thought groups:

- prominence[1]
- stressed syllables within prominent words
- vowel peaks within stressed syllables
- consonants and consonant clusters
- naturally occurring phonological processes (e.g., deletion, linking, assimilation) that commonly occur across word boundaries but only within thought groups
- volume, pacing, and the rhythm of spoken English
- intonation

REFLECTIVE BREAK

- What does the following imply with respect to pronunciation teaching?

Thought groups represent a requisite phonological context for all components of English pronunciation. If we ask what comes first— the prominent word, a stressed syllable, or any of the other bulleted items listed above—the answer is always the same. The thought group comes first.

---

[1] Other terms sometimes used include *focal stress* and *sentence stress*.

A Familiar Illustration

Generally speaking, pauses and the pulses of thought groups between them serve as cues for listeners to more easily recognize grammatical units such as phrases and clauses within longer stretches of speech. Consider, for example, this familiar line from John F. Kennedy's 1961 U.S. presidential inaugural address:

> *"Ask not what your country can do for you; ask what you can do for your country."*

As a quick YouTube search confirms, Kennedy divided this 17-word stretch into at least three, perhaps four, thought groups as follows (parentheses indicate an optional or indistinct pause):

> // Ask not // what your country can do for you //
> ask what you (//) can do for your country //

Ask not—well, that's a thought group. Kennedy paused for a brief though perceptible moment both immediately before and after it. *Ask not* also happens to be a verb phrase and the stem of an imperative sentence. *What your country can do for you* is a noun clause that serves to complete the preceding verb phrase. Notice that each thought group corresponds with a coherent grammatical function even though it does not necessarily constitute a full sentence on its own. The pattern of using two thought groups to express a fuller idea is repeated with the next phrase, *ask what you,* and its resolution, *can do for your country.* The speaker could have used fewer thought groups or even a single one for the entire set of 17 words; however, the impact on listeners might have been less memorable. As a seasoned politician well aware of the persuasive power of language, Kennedy was using the phenomenon of thought grouping to guide listeners for the purpose of maximum audience impact. Notice, too, that Kennedy projected some words within thought groups more forcefully than others. These more forcefully projected words are called *prominent* words. They may be represented as follows:

> // Ask **<u>not</u>** // what your country can do for **<u>you</u>** //
> ask what **<u>you</u>** (//) can do for your **<u>country</u>** //

I use bolding and underlining to call attention to the speaker's applications of prominence, including increased volume and vowel clarity. The point to notice is that words made prominent in a speaker's delivery, and the characteristics of English pronunciation with which they correspond, all happen within the phonological context of the thought group.

REFLECTIVE BREAK

- Besides the John F. Kennedy quotation, can you think of any other well-known quotes that might be useful for illustrating thought groups?

- How might any of the following conditions impact the process of thought grouping: fatigue, language proficiency, nervousness, anxiety, elation, anger, inebriation.

How Do Thought Groups Work?

Speakers of English use pauses and the thought groups between them as tools for guiding listeners toward fuller understanding (Gilbert, 2009). Although there are no rigid rules for exactly where the pauses straddling thought groups tend to appear, there are some general parameters worth introducing in language classrooms. Pauses work best when they occur at locations that enhance meaningful communication. Further, the meaning the speaker is trying to convey is pivotal. Typically, pauses are not inserted between thought groups randomly; there is an internal logic to the system. A central principle is that the insertion of pauses between thought groups depends on the speaker's pragmatic intent (the idea or effect the speaker is trying to convey; Cauldwell, 2002). For example, consider Excerpt 2 from the Airplane Aisle Incident.

> ### The Airplane Aisle Incident: Excerpt 2
>
> opened the overhead compartment and was waiting my turn to leave the plane in back of me I heard a noise that didn't sound right when I turned I saw an older man was falling into a woman behind him

It would be very unlikely to insert pauses following the words *leave* and *me* because doing so would group the words *the plane in back of me* into a single thought group. Though an identically worded thought group might work perfectly well in a different context, here it would only confuse the listener (e.g., Was there another plane?). Because minds operate faster than organs of speech, the speaker was already anticipating the subsequent sections of her narrative. By pausing momentarily after the word *plane* prior to saying *in back of me I heard a noise*, the speaker's pragmatic intent is made clear and a listener can more easily follow her story. Such subtle differences in meaning are easier for listeners to recognize if the speaker is already providing relevant cues through the process of thought grouping.

As long as pause locations succeed in getting the speaker's intended meaning across, there is flexibility in the system. The process of thought grouping is sensitive to the dynamic, subtle, interpersonal contexts within which speakers and listeners interact (Brazil, 1994). Finally, speakers typically insert pauses to form thought groups comprising semantically and grammatically coherent word clusters (Celce-Murcia, Brinton, Goodwin, & Griner, 2010).

How Long Is a Thought Group?

Though a thought group can be as brief as a single word, listeners tend to perceive those of more than 7–9 words as rather long. Anything more than about 10–12 words, though certainly possible, becomes increasingly problematic for listeners. Most of us probably know speakers of English whose sheer quantity of delivery in number of words between pauses can sometimes overwhelm listeners. Though we normally refer to such speakers as "fast talkers," the problematic feature of their speaking style is less a matter of the velocity of their organs of speech and more a consequence of infrequent pauses in their streams of speech. Infrequent pausing results in longish, poorly delineated thought groups that listeners may have trouble following and may perceive as uncomfortably rapid speech. The optimum size of a thought group (i.e., the number of words or syllables it contains) depends on intuitive decisions usually made beneath the level of a speaker's conscious attention. When necessary, however, speakers are capable of controlling the process of thought grouping.

How Do Thought Groups Benefit Learners?

As language proficiency advances, a significant challenge learners face is to begin to express themselves in longer speaking turns made up of consecutive thought groups (still separated by intermittent pauses) that are organized sensibly and focused on related themes. In fact, length of speaking turn is one of the primary features differentiating levels of oral proficiency in English. Eventually, advanced ESL speakers reach a point when they are able to converse in an interactive conversation through their use of multiple thought groups of related content during individual speaking turns. To help learners continue to move in this direction while also focusing on pronunciation, an appropriate teaching strategy is to build awareness of what thought groups are and how speakers can use them to be more clearly understood. As the earlier identical-prepositions activity illustrates, we can foster such awareness from the very earliest stages of language instruction. Here are some objectives for students:

- to become more mindful with respect to the process of thought grouping
- to fine-tune awareness until the process becomes second nature
- to develop intuition about when to let the process operate automatically and when to shift to more deliberate control

Definitions

Grant (2007) writes that "a thought group is a group of words that naturally go together" (p. 125). Celce-Murcia et al. (2010) define a thought group as a "discrete stretch of speech that forms a semantically and grammatically coherent segment of discourse" (p. 221).

Teaching Pronunciation

- What does the following add to a working definition of thought groups?

  You should think of the [thought group] as the basic building block of spoken English. When language is written or printed, it appears to the eye as divided up into "words." When it is spoken it is heard by the ear as divided up into [thought groups]. Notice that the sounds that make up a [thought group] are usually run together in the way we are accustomed to thinking of the separate sounds of single words as being run together. (Brazil, 1994, p. 7)

For learners who are ready for fuller discussion, we might add the following:

- A thought group is something a speaker creates; it is not something formed automatically.

- Some speakers are better than others at thought grouping.

- Thought grouping is a central phonological feature that English language learners can learn to work with effectively.

- A thought group corresponds with an internal rhythmic structure that can be manipulated by speakers to good effect.

- If not a complete pause, there is a holding of a thought group's final stressed syllable before the next thought group begins (e.g., the single syllable in the word *seats* in the thought group // everyone got out of their **seats** //).

- A thought group usually contains one particularly salient word (e.g., // in **back** of me //; // he fully **recovered** //).

- The thought group's most salient word will contain a primary stressed syllable on which the speaker's voice lingers. Further, the vowel of this particular syllable will be more forcefully projected (louder) and will take a bit longer to enunciate than the vowels of the syllables around it (e.g., the vowel of *back* in the thought group // in **back** of me //; the vowel of the syllable *cov* in the thought group // he fully re**cov**ered //).

- Primary stressed syllables tend to coincide with the initiation of a distinct pitch movement (e.g., a slight drop or rise in pitch).

What Else Do Learners Need to Know?

Once such preliminary descriptions have been established, here are some related topics worth introducing to learners gradually over time:

- **Awareness**: A priority is to build awareness of the use of pauses to delineate thought groups.

- **Linking**: Words within a thought group are closely linked together (e.g., "What is the matter?" → "Smatter?"), whereas words across thought group boundaries are not.

- **Internal structure**: A thought group usually corresponds with a grammatical structure (e.g., a noun or verb phrase, a prepositional phrase, a relative clause).

- **Speaking rate**: Generally, a slower rate of speech leads to more, and more clearly delineated, thought groups.

- **Length**: Faster speech corresponds with fewer pauses and longer thought groups containing more words.

- **Intelligibility**: Because slower speech corresponds with more thought groups, listeners usually find speech that contains more frequent pauses and a higher number of recognizable thought groups easier to understand.

  — **Limits to slower speech**: However, one's rate of speech can become excessively slow if there are just too many thought group divisions. Goodwin (2001) explains that a common error of "less fluent speakers is pausing too frequently, thereby overloading the listener with too many breaks to process the discourse effectively" (p. 119).

- **Goldilocks principle**: An appropriate long-term strategy is to develop a moderate rate of speech (i.e., not too fast [too few thought groups] and not too slow [too many thought groups]) to be optimally intelligible.

- **Register**: More formal registers of speech tend to correspond with more frequent pauses and a corresponding larger number of thought groups containing fewer words (e.g., political speeches, job interviews).

- **Time to monitor**: Pauses provide ESL/EFL speakers with more time to self-monitor and make appropriate choices.

REFLECTIVE BREAK

- In your own words, how would you define *thought groups* for a class of ESL/EFL learners?

- What resources might you use to illustrate the process of thought grouping?

- How would you respond to a skeptical learner who asked, "Why are we learning about thought groups?"

Conclusion

The purpose of developing a moderate speaking rate is so that ESL/EFL speakers can be more clearly understood by listeners. A teacher's challenge is to provide opportunities for learners to incorporate an appropriate degree of pausing in their speech, at locations that make sense, so that learners' speech consists of thought groups containing reasonable numbers of words. Given the general benefits associated with a moderate rate of speech, it is profitable for teachers to guide learners in the use of thought groups for more effective communication. Ideally, students will learn to adjust their rates of speech to best fit the communicative situation. To do so, pronunciation instruction should prioritize opportunities to learn about the process of thought grouping at all levels of speaking proficiency through awareness raising, direct instruction, and plenty of practice opportunities.

The four chapters to follow offer a practical model for teaching pronunciation reflecting these priorities. The model's purposes are to illustrate instructional possibilities grounded in contemporary theory (e.g., Cauldwell, 2002; Dickerson, 2010) and practice (e.g., Gilbert, 2009; Grant, 2007; Morley, 1994) and to serve as a starting point from which teachers may modify some of the ideas offered to best fit learners' needs. Chapter 2 focuses on preplanning tasks teachers need to complete prior to classroom teaching. The tasks center on finding and organizing appropriate language samples to use in class. Chapters 3–5 discuss eight other important facets of pronunciation worth teaching once learners are aware of, and have begun to work with, the process of thought grouping. These additional facets are prominence, featured words, rehearsal strategies, syllables, word stress, vowels, body language, and consonants.

2

What Teachers Need to Do

To get ready to teach pronunciation, a teacher's first task is to locate a good selection of language samples that will be appropriate for the proficiency level of the class. Though a combination of both written and oral language samples is recommended, in this book I focus on ways of working with written samples because written texts serve as centerpieces for ESL/EFL teaching in most classrooms worldwide. If the course is already focused on pronunciation, the students' textbook may contain plenty of promising language samples. Many teachers, however, want to be able to include at least some attention to pronunciation in courses that are not pronunciation focused. Some very good news is that even in more broadly focused courses, potentially useful language samples are all around us.

An appropriate language sample for teaching pronunciation may be as uncomplicated as an introductory dialogue from a beginning-level EFL text or as challenging as a transcript of an academic lecture from an advanced-level listening for academic purposes text. All such materials can be useful, depending on the characteristics of the language sample and learners' level of proficiency. We should also think about the length, in number of words, of a potential language sample. For courses geared toward lower proficiency levels, texts between 50 and 170 words are probably long enough. This would be the typical length of dialogues and paragraphs often featured in lower-level EFL texts. The Airplane Aisle Incident narrative is just under 190 words and suggests that texts between 170 and 250 words are appropriate for intermediate-level classes. Students at high-intermediate and advanced levels of proficiency may work with language samples that are considerably longer. Higher-level courses may also begin to incorporate a mix of written texts accompanied by audio recordings (e.g., transcripts of interviews, radio broadcasts, lectures). Here are some steps to follow prior to pronunciation teaching:

- Find language samples of appropriate length that meet learners' needs.

- Include samples of written language that feature at least some characteristics of spoken discourse.

- Consider both commercially published and self-generated language samples.

- Include source materials from different media (e.g., books, Internet, radio, TV).

- Prioritize language samples featured in the class textbook.

In addition to written texts, samples of spoken language generated live in the classroom can also be used. Approaches to language teaching, such as the direct method, language experience approach, and Community Language Learning, feature procedures for transcribing samples of spoken language generated live in the classroom. More conventionally, most ESL and EFL textbooks, even those designed to teach integrated skills, reading, writing, or grammar, include either scripted simulations of speech or prose selections that can be very effective as supports for pronunciation teaching. Radio podcasts such as National Public Radio's *Fresh Air* and *StoryCorps* are appropriate as long as the content has been screened for suitability. Alternatively, it is a good idea to sometimes use language samples you have generated on your own (e.g., the Airline Aisle Incident). In sum, the first step in preparing to teach pronunciation is to locate an appropriate number of language samples (e.g., one or more per week) that are relevant to students' level of proficiency, of sufficient length, and interesting enough to both capture and maintain student interest.

REFLECTIVE BREAK

- Which of the following do you think are more important to include as core language samples when teaching pronunciation: dialogues, monologues, narratives; scripted, semiscripted, or authentic language samples; excerpts from lectures, podcasts, textbooks, screenplays, novels, TV interviews, radio shows, EAP listening materials?

- In an ESL/EFL textbook you are currently using, locate two to three sections that provide potentially useful language samples. What characteristics are you considering?

Preparing Language Samples

Once you have identified a language sample, you need to decide if it will be more helpful as either a *general* or a *core* language sample. General language samples can be used as they are. Typically, these are brief sections from students' textbooks used to introduce, illustrate, and reinforce the concept of thought grouping or other pronunciation features. In contrast, core samples require more preparation because they will serve as centerpieces for instruction. A large concern is that core language samples need to be reformatted ahead of time. As you experienced with the Airplane Aisle Incident narrative, the idea is to reformat core samples so that all punctuation has been removed. In most instances, this means retyping them and saving them as electronic files. Language samples from a textbook also need to be retyped and reformatted; otherwise the removal of punctuation is impossible. Because students will be marking them up extensively, double-spacing is recommended. The remainder of this book prioritizes core language samples for purposes of pronunciation teaching. It is worth keeping in mind, however, that general samples from students' textbooks are also useful. In short, once core language samples have been identified, the teacher needs to retype them in order to render them punctuation-free.

Introducing the Language Sample in Class

Once a core language sample is in place, the next question is: How will I present it to the class? Sometimes a combination of audio and written versions is needed, although for shorter and less complicated texts a teacher might simply read the language sample aloud to the class. For teachers interested in exposing learners to the voices of different English speakers, audio recordings may also be used. For most activities a written version is required because students will be analyzing it closely to be able to work on pronunciation features. Some possibilities for presenting language samples include the following:

- Everyone gets a photocopy (preferred).
- A copy is projected at the front of the room (e.g., overhead, PowerPoint).
- Students create their own written version through teacher-fronted listening dictation or dicto-comp activities.[2]
- Other classroom procedures such as information gaps, jigsaw procedures, strip sentences, and cloze exercises may also be used.

REFLECTIVE BREAK

- Why might punctuation-free language samples be more useful than conventional texts?
- What would be your preferred way of presenting a core language sample in class?

---

[2] Dicto-comp is a technique in which the teacher reads a language sample aloud and students write out what they understand and remember while trying to keep as close as possible to the original.

Conclusion

This chapter focused on tasks a classroom teacher needs to complete ahead of time to prepare for pronunciation teaching. The three tasks are to (1) locate language samples relevant to learners' needs, (2) create versions that are punctuation-free, and (3) decide how to present them in class. These preparatory steps are necessary so that students will be able to work closely with useful samples of English as a basis for pronunciation work. When looking for appropriate language samples, the best ones are written texts that reflect at least some of the characteristics of spoken English. The next chapter explains how students can be guided in the productive use of such core language samples.

3

What Students Need to Do

This chapter discusses the primary tasks we will be asking students to complete as a necessary foundation for work on pronunciation. As outlined in Chapter 1, thought groups constitute the phonological environment within which pronunciation happens. By beginning with the process of thought grouping first, teachers can then use thought groups as the anchor for teaching pronunciation. Lane (2010) suggests that both teachers and students find the process of thought grouping to be a particularly accessible pronunciation feature, one that can be taught successfully in many kinds of ESL/EFL classrooms. Both Brazil (1994) and Dickerson (2010) recommend that the process of thought grouping needs to be our starting point if learners are going to perceive later pronunciation topics as making sense.

REFLECTIVE BREAK

- Why might the process of thought grouping be worth teaching across different proficiency levels?

- What are some ways of focusing learners' attention on thought groups?

Learning Objectives

The first learning objective is for learners to be able to identify thought groups in the core language sample presented to them. To prepare students, the teacher needs to (1) define and teach what thought groups are, (2) provide illustrations, (3) demonstrate how and why speakers use thought groups, (4) explain and illustrate strategies for locating thought groups in a written text, (5) show learners how to insert slash marks to signal pauses between thought groups, and (6) provide a printed language sample so that students' work can begin.

Once this preparatory work is completed and students have access to a core language sample, the teacher can ask them to locate as many thought groups as possible in the sample. Pair or small-group work is particularly useful at this stage. To keep track of the thought groups they find, students should use an erasable pencil or pen to mark boundaries between thought groups, as illustrated in Chapter 1. While engaged in these tasks, students will likely turn to you often with a lot of questions. Once a sufficient number of thought groups have been identified, students may move on to rehearsing the language sample aloud in pairs. Their charge is to practice saying at least a dozen of the thought groups aloud several times each while learning to insert pauses between them.

An Application Task

Here is an example of the learning tasks just described. Your challenge is to try to figure out what the speaker's thought groups might have been while attending to some of the nuances in meaning the speaker may have intended to convey.

Identifying Thought Groups in the Airplane Aisle Incident[3]

Directions: Insert double slash marks to indicate likely pause locations in the speaker's stream of speech.

Example:

the plane landed // the cabin lights turned on // everyone got out of their seats // I stepped into the aisle // opened the overhead compartment // and was waiting my turn to leave the plane //

- in back of me I heard a noise that didn't sound right when I turned I saw an older man was falling into a woman behind him

- he looked scared his face was stone white I didn't think he was breathing

- I yelled for help and then a couple of us moved into action the first thing I did was to get the people behind me to back away by this point most of the aisle had cleared

- so we were able to stretch him out on the floor I heard someone say we have to get him out of the plane so I grabbed his legs this tall guy grabbed his shoulders and we carried him off I know CPR so I cleared a space made sure everyone else was out of the way

- fortunately when it was all over he fully recovered seemed to be fine

The task you have just completed illustrates one of the most important tools for effective communication in English. It is intended to serve as a prototype for designing ESL/EFL classroom activities you will be able to build upon and further develop on your own.

---

[3] See the Appendix for answer key for this and later application tasks.

- What difficulties did you have in completing the thought group identification task?

- How might you modify such a task to better suit learners' needs?

Prominence

Once learners are comfortable working with thought groups, the second feature of pronunciation to teach is prominence. Notice that discussions of prominence are meaningless until an appreciation for thought grouping has first been established. An awareness of thought groups establishes the landscape for pronunciation work, but prominence is the anchor of the rhythm system of spoken English (Hahn, 2004). The task to set before students is to ask them to identify prominent words for the thought groups with which they have already been working. What they need to know is that some of the words within a thought group, and always at least one word, stand out in relation to the other words surrounding them. Consider the word in bold print for each of the following thought groups:

// sorry to **bother** you //

// don't **mention** it //

// this is **fantastic** news //

Prominence refers to the tendency in spoken English for one word within a thought group to stand out in a listener's perceptual field. It is the word that a speaker "punches out" more forcefully (i.e., with more acoustic energy) relative to its neighboring words. A prominent word is a bit louder in the speech stream and therefore will be more noticeable. Another essential point to teach is that within a prominent word of more than one syllable, it is specifically the word's primary stressed syllable that most bears the prominence feature (e.g., the first syllable of ***bother***, the first syllable of ***mention***, the second syllable of *fantastic* in the examples above). The vowels of these particular syllables are not only louder, but they also take a bit longer to enunciate. As Goodwin (2001) explains, "within each thought group, there is generally one *prominent* element, a particular syllable [within a prominent word] that is emphasized" (p. 119). This happens because the speaker's voice lingers a bit longer for the peak vowel of a prominent word's primary stressed syllable (Lane, 2010).

REFLECTIVE BREAK

- In the following dialogue, why does Justin's use of the word *you* receive prominence whereas David's initial use of the same word does not? Also, why is *hated* a prominent word in Justin's final speaking turn?

  David: *Hey! Good to **see** you. How **are** you?*

  Justin: *I'm doing well. How are **you**?*

  David: *Everything's good. I saw Pat yesterday. She said you just got back from a cruise.*

  Justin: *Oh, don't remind me. I **hated** it. Too much food, too many people, and the cabins were tiny. If you ever go on cruise, make sure you have a good book.*

In general, speakers use prominent words as navigational cues for directing (and refocusing) conversations while the trajectory of the conversation is still unfolding (Gilbert, 2009). This second feature of pronunciation is highly sensitive to contextual considerations and a speaker's pragmatic intent (Cauldwell, 2002). For this reason, it is really not very useful for English language learners to examine or discuss prominence with sentences or thought groups out of context, a pervasive and persistent problem with many ESL/EFL textbooks. Prominence also allows speakers to spice up what they have to say. When Justin used *hated* as a prominent word, its introduction was unexpected and the tone of the conversation shifted.

Teaching Pronunciation

To prepare students to work with prominence, there are four things a teacher needs to do:

- Define and teach what prominence is.
- Provide plenty of illustrations.
- Demonstrate how and why speakers use prominence within thought groups.
- Explain and illustrate strategies for locating prominent words.

Once students seem ready, they can begin to build upon their work with the same language sample they already divided into thought groups. Their new task is to locate at least one prominent word for each of the sample's thought groups. An easy way to set prominent words apart is to circle each one. Student pairs or small groups can discuss and compare their efforts.

REFLECTIVE BREAK

- Return to your previous work (earlier in this chapter) on the identification of thought groups in the Airplane Aisle Incident narrative. This time, circle at least one prominent word for each of the thought groups you identified. (The Appendix provides an answer key.)

After prominent words have been identified, the activity of rehearsing the language sample aloud can resume. This time students' rehearsals may focus on prominence within thought groups. Their new task is to use increased volume and vowel lengthening as signals of prominence.

For students who are ready for a slightly fuller explanation, you can point out the special role played by the primary stressed syllable of prominent words. This particular syllable not only is a bit louder and lasts a bit longer than other syllables, but also coincides with a perceptible change in tone. Tone shifts in English (either a slight rise or a slight fall of a speaker's voice) begin on the vowel of the prominent word's most strongly stressed syllable. To review: the three pronunciation features used to express prominence are (1) increased volume,

(2) a lengthening of the prominent word's primary stressed syllable, and (3) a tone shift either up or down on the stressed syllable.

Featured Words

After students have been working with thought groups and prominence during the first two sets of pronunciation tasks, they may begin to notice that some thought groups contain more than just one salient word. As this point (and especially when learners begin to ask about it) you can explain that if there are multiple words receiving stress within a thought group, English speakers tend to pronounce one of the words a bit more forcefully than the others. As discussed earlier, the one most forcefully pronounced is the prominent word; other more lightly stressed words are called *featured* words. Here is an example:

// **I** like buying used cars <u>**too**</u> //

Prominence falls on *too*, whereas *I* is a less strongly stressed featured word. Having the opportunity to discuss featured words provides opportunities to both reinforce and more fully define how prominent words and thought groups function. It is only by understanding these three pronunciation features in relation to each other that students gain a clearer understanding of the respective roles each plays in English pronunciation. Here is another example.

// there are literally **hundreds** of <u>cities</u> that we could have <u>visited</u> //

In this 11-word example, *hundreds* is the prominent word, but both *cities* and *visited* also receive some stress. Though one could argue that *literally* might also carry stress, it is more likely that it would remain unstressed in order to leave plenty of acoustic space for prominence to be placed on the word immediately following it. For teaching purposes, we can refer to words such as *cities* and *visited* as featured words, whereas prominence is reserved for words such as *hundreds* in this example. As far as rules for which word is most prominent in relation to the others, that depends on the speaker's pragmatic intent. A full context of communication needs to be available for the meaning a speaker is trying to convey to become apparent.

- Given the discussion so far, what does Cauldwell (2002) mean when he proposes that thought grouping, prominence, and other rhythmic features of spoken English are necessarily "speaker-controlled, purpose-driven, interactive, co-operative, context-related, and context-changing" (p. 2)?

As teachers, we need to realize that speakers use similar phonological features to signal both featured words and prominent words. These features are volume (they are more loudly produced) and time (they take longer to say). In the case of prominent words, there may also be a slight rise or a slight fall in the speaker's voice, coinciding with the primary stressed syllable. These characteristics tend to fall on content-laden words as determined not by grammatical category or some implicit characteristic of stress-timing in English, but by the meaning focus of the speakers' conversational flow (Cauldwell, 2002). Also, a simple guideline is that there are more featured words than prominent words in English speech. As with the phenomenon of primary stressed syllables, an intonation change within a thought group normally initiates on the primary stressed syllable of a prominent word; see the underlined syllables below:

// and it would **rea**lly be a disaster (//) if my **step**father showed up //

Further, new information tends to be featured prominently, and old information does not. Imagine that the following two thought groups are spoken by the same person.

1. // I can think of **three** of her **cousins** who I'd **really** like to **invite** to the **wedding** //

2. // and I can think of **three** of **my** cousins who I really **don't** want to invite at **all** //

Notice that Item 1 features the word *cousins*, but for Item 2 a listener would already realize that *cousins* are part of the topic of conversation; therefore the same word no longer needs to be featured. As shared information previously established, *cousins* may now move to the background of the conversation. For Items 3–5, appearing in the following Reflective Break, consider how a series of prominent words would emerge in reference to other family members if the same speaker were to continue voicing his or her concerns:

REFLECTIVE BREAK

- For Items 3–5, see if you can figure out which five words (only) would likely be the prominent words. When you locate them, circle each one:

    3. // but I want my sisters to be there // no matter what //

    4. // I hope my father stays away //

    5. // it would really be a disaster (//) if my stepfather showed up //

- Now, provide some justification for why those five words would be prominent.

Are there any other words that might be featured but not prominent?

In Item 5, *stepfather* is prominent as a result of the speaker wanting to contrast it with the use of *father* in Item 4. Generally, words used in contrast to something previously mentioned tend to serve as prominent words. We can simultaneously define and illustrate this principle of *contrastive stress* by imagining that a single speaker is contrasting the words *new* and *old*:

// <u>new</u> information tends to be featured //
// while <u>old</u> information does not //

Finally, words used emphatically also tend to be prominent, such as *don't* and *all* in this sample from Item 2 above:

// who I really <u>don't</u> want to invite at <u>all</u> //

There is a similar use of emphatic stress on the word *really* in Item 5. Although this is not an exhausted list of phonological conditions that lead to prominent and other featured words, the list is more

Teaching Pronunciation

than enough to point ESL/EFL learners in the right direction in their analysis of language samples.

Recapping the Learning Tasks So Far

By now, students have spent considerable time with the core language sample and have come to know it well. They have identified its thought groups, prominent words, and featured words. Eventually, we also want students to discuss the content of the selection more extemporaneously as well as the elements of pronunciation they are noticing. We certainly want to complement the types of rehearsal activities emphasized here with more fluency-building ESL/EFL activities such as discussions, games, role-plays, mock interviews, simulations, and so forth. By calling attention to a manageable number of core pronunciation features, however, teachers can better prepare learners to apply such features when speaking extemporaneously. It is up to the teacher to decide how long students will continue to work with the same language sample or when it might be time to introduce a different one and begin the process again. For simplicity of presentation, throughout the remainder of the book I assume that subsequent stages will continue to make use of the same language sample.

REFLECTIVE BREAK

- What are some advantages of continuing to work with a single language sample over the course of several classes? Some disadvantages?

- What criteria would you apply for deciding when to move students on to a new language sample?

Rehearsal

Rehearsal procedures represent a culmination of students' work on pronunciation so far. These are opportunities to integrate and consolidate knowledge and to grow more comfortable with the pronunciation features being introduced. When rehearsing, students' tasks are (a) to practice the language sample aloud while applying what they have learned, (b) to delineate thought groups with pauses, and (c) to modulate their voices to signal both prominent and featured words. The in-class use of audio recorders is optional but very useful in settings where students really want to focus on improvements in pronunciation. Recordings of students' speech make it possible for students to analyze their efforts closely, either individually or in teams.

Read-and-Look-Up

When working with students of adequate proficiency, I lead discussion of how and why professional actors prepare for performances by rehearsing written scripts aloud along with some of the strategies acting coaches use to support actors. Eventually, and across all proficiency levels, the *Read-and-Look-Up* (RALU) procedure can serve as a model for student rehearsals. The RALU procedure is similar to the way a professional actor might work one-on-one with a speech coach. In RALU, speakers always have the text in front of them. Their task is to work with the text but to learn to look away from it and into their partner's eyes (ideally) whenever words are leaving their mouths. Speakers who are hesitant to make direct eye contact have the option of looking in some other direction as long as it is up and away from the page. The listener's role is to be encouraging and supportive. RALU taps into short-term memory as students intermittently prepare what they are about to say, usually just one to three thought groups at a time, and then look away from the page before speaking them aloud. As familiarity with the material grows, learners are able to say more consecutive thought groups at a time. RALU dovetails nicely with the learning preferences of many cultural groups, particularly those who come from more traditional styles of schooling (e.g., in Asia, the Middle East, Africa).

Once RALU rehearsals begin, the teacher's role is to arrange the class into pairs, remind students to focus on thought groups and prominent words, and explain that they will be taking turns in the roles of *actor rehearsing* and *supportive coach*. Morley (1994) recommends additional modifications such as strong vigorous practice, exaggerated practice, self-monitoring, slow-motion and half-speed practice, loop ("broken record") practice, whispering practice, as well as mirror and video practice. If students are going to use audio recorders, it is a good idea to discuss some of the advantages of working with them for self-assessment. Once students are ready, their tasks are to rehearse the language sample aloud multiple times while delineating thought groups, prominence, and featured words.

> ## REFLECTIVE BREAK
>
> - What difficulties might students have with RALU procedures?
>
> - What are some advantages (and disadvantages) of having students audio-record their rehearsals?
>
> - What learning tasks would you design for students listening to recordings of their own speech?

Conclusion

This chapter introduced the central teaching procedures and learning tasks featured in the book. These included the use of a core language sample as a basis for pronunciation work as well as several tasks for learners to complete that ask them to identify thought groups, prominent words, and featured words. The final section illustrated some options for getting learners to rehearse the core language sample aloud while using it in ways similar to how actors prepare for theatrical performances. By placing thought groups, prominent words, and featured words at the center of pronunciation teaching, teachers give students opportunities to focus their energies in a direction that will really make a difference in the quality of their speech (Cauldwell, 2002) and the degree to which listeners will understand them (Hahn, 2004). Likewise, teachers will be structuring the limited time usually available for pronunciation teaching on pivotal rather than peripheral concerns (Dickerson, 2010).

4

Syllables and Individual Words

Chapter 3 established a landscape for pronunciation teaching. Its primary feature is the process of thought grouping, a topic tied to the roles of prominence and featured words in the pronunciation of English. Building upon these relatively broad components, this chapter describes how characteristics of individual words interact with thought groups and prominence. These characteristics include a prominent word's total number of syllables, the location of its primary stressed syllable, and patterns of word stress. Just as discussions of prominence are meaningless until an appreciation for the process of thought grouping has first been established, the characteristics of individual words discussed in this chapter are better appreciated once the construct of prominence has been established.

Number of Syllables Within a Word

To know how to pronounce a word in English, the speaker needs to get its number of syllables right. One reason is that listeners anticipate hearing the right number of syllables arranged in a particular pattern of word-level stress (Field, 2005). Another reason is that getting the number of syllables right lays a necessary foundation for the speaker to also be able to (a) stress the word's primary syllable, (b) produce the vowel sound of that particular syllable with at least a threshold level of precision, and (c) leave the word's remaining syllables unstressed or only lightly stressed, as appropriate. For example, in the unusually long word *overgeneralization*, there are eight syllables. Its seventh syllable is primary stressed, and that is the particular syllable English language listeners expect to hear most clearly.

						/	
o	ver	gen	er	al	i	**za**	tion
1	2	3	4	5	6	**7**	8

When learning to pronounce a new word, students need to be aware of its number of syllables. Being able to figure out a word's syllable count is especially important for prominent words because those are the ones listeners depend upon most. To foster such awareness, the teacher needs to define what syllables are, provide examples, and illustrate that there is usually one vowel for each syllable of an English word. Although these are relatively easy ideas for students to understand conceptually, it takes focused practice before understanding begins to make a difference in pronunciation. As the next steps in working with the core language sample, some learning tasks for students include focusing on the prominent words they have already identified and figuring out the number of syllables for at least 12 of them.

REFLECTIVE BREAK

- What are some tips and strategies you would share with students for learning to identify the number of syllables in a word?

Celce-Murcia et al. (2010), Goodwin (2014), and Grant (2007) provide many classroom activities designed to focus learners' attention on figuring out the number of syllables in English words. Working with such resources, I usually ask students to create a list of prominent words with their number of syllables indicated. During rehearsal activities, students can be asked to practice saying prominent words aloud while focusing on getting their number of syllables right.

Primary Stressed Syllables

Along with identifying the number of syllables in a word, an equally important step is to locate the word's primary stressed syllable. As before, the priority should be prominent words within thought groups. In preparation, the teacher might consult resources such as Dauer (1983, pp. 67–69) and Celce-Murcia et al. (2010, pp. 187–194), which provide accessible rules for determining primary stressed syllable locations. For example, the primary stressed syllable for words ending in the suffixes *–tion*, *–sion*, *–ic*, *–ical*, *–ity*, and *–graphy* is almost always the syllable immediate before the suffix (e.g., elec<u>**tri**</u>city, edu<u>**ca**</u>tion). Also, two-syllable words such as *permit* and *conduct*, which can function as either nouns or verbs, carry primary stress on their first syllable when functioning as nouns and on their second syllable when functioning as verbs.

> ## REFLECTIVE BREAK
>
> - What are some other rules for identifying a word's primary stressed syllable?
>
> - In your experience, do learners find such rules helpful?

To introduce the topic, teachers need to define what primary stressed syllables are while demonstrating that these particular syllables are a bit louder and take a bit longer to pronounce. This provides an opportunity to make connections with several of the concepts featured in Chapter 3. Just as there may be both prominent words and featured words within a single thought group, there may be both primary stressed and secondary stressed syllables within a single word. Revisiting our earlier example, *overgeneralization* receives primary stress on its seventh syllable while both its first and third syllables receive secondary stress.

\\		\\				/	
o	ver	**gen**	er	al	i	**za**	tion
1	**2**	**3**	**4**	**5**	**6**	**7**	**8**

REFLECTIVE BREAK

- How might you explain the following analogies to students? What concepts are they intended to convey?

    a. Prominent words are to featured words as primary stressed syllables are to secondary stressed syllables.

    b. Prominent words are to thought groups as primary stressed syllables are to individual words.

What students need to realize is that speakers who consistently get primary stressed syllables right are easier for listeners to understand. When students are ready, their next task in working with the core language sample is to insert an accent mark (e.g., /) precisely above the primary stressed syllable of each prominent word. In pairs or small groups, learners can be asked to compare their efforts and to continue rehearsing the language sample aloud while focusing on primary stressed syllables. To make these prominent syllables clear, the pronunciation features students should be applying are increased volume and vowel lengthening.

Word Stress Patterns

Once learners begin to see that primary stressed syllables distinguish the prominent words within thought groups, there needs to be an easy way to talk about primary stressed syllables in class. This stage is important because stress patterns of particular words will be easier to notice, talk about, and remember if everyone has shared conventions for talking about them. Students have already identified the number of syllables of prominent words, and they have located the words' primary stressed syllables. The next task is to teach learners to assign an easy-to-remember label for the stress pattern of prominent words. To accomplish this, I introduce an uncomplicated two-digit numbering system (see Murphy, 2004). For example, the word *communication* is a 5-4 word. This label means that *communication* is a 5-syllable word with primary stress on its 4th syllable. On the other hand, the word *father* is a 2-1 word, a 2-syllable word with primary stress on its 1st syllable.

The system provides a convenient shorthand for identifying both the number of syllables in a word and the location of its primary stressed syllable. I find that students pick the system up quickly.

REFLECTIVE BREAK

- Why might it be useful to use such a numeric system when teaching the pronunciation of individual words?

- How might we modify the system to make it applicable to words such as *economic*, *methodology*, *and education*, which have a secondary stressed syllable as well as a primary stressed syllable?

When learners return to the core language sample, they can begin to assign numeric labels for each of the sample's prominent words. Once established as a set of shared conventions, the labeling system is a useful tool for classroom discussion whenever questions about patterns of word stress arise.

Conclusion

This chapter built upon the broader focus of Chapters 1–3 by focusing on syllables and patterns of word stress of prominent words. By this point, students' oral rehearsals of the core language sample have expanded to include five essential features of English pronunciation: thought groups, prominence, featured words, syllable counts, and the location of primary stressed syllables. This chapter also introduced a handy two-digit numbering system intended to make it easier for students and teachers to discuss word stress patterns in class. Parallels were drawn between the operation of prominent words within thought groups and how primary stressed syllables operate within individual words. Although the topics featured in Chapter 4 may not be as broadly applicable in ESL/EFL classrooms as were the topics treated in earlier chapters, any course featuring attention to vocabulary learning might benefit from students having access to shared conventions for talking about the stress patterns of individual words. Chapter 5 continues to build upon these themes.

Vowels, Consonants, and Body Language

The first two topics covered in this final chapter are intended to be featured in pronunciation-centered courses. The chapter's third topic, body language, has broader implications for ESL/EFL pronunciation teaching. Minimally, students will need to be aware of how thought groups, prominence, and primary stressed syllables contribute to the pronunciation of English in order to more fully appreciate how vowels, consonants, and body language operate.

Vowel Sounds

Learners of English need to know about vowel sounds because these serve as the virtual peaks of primary stressed syllables. As such, there are direct connections between vowels and the clear pronunciation of stressed syllables, prominent words, and thought groups. When combined, these are the four elements that contribute most to the clarity of a speaker's pronunciation (Gilbert, 2009; Hahn, 2004). A premise of this chapter is that if students are unfamiliar with English vowels and consonants, then these topics need to be taught in class.

> ### REFLECTIVE BREAK
>
> - How would you begin to introduce ESL/EFL students to vowel and/or consonant sounds?
>
> - What are some related classroom activities you would use?

If you are new to this area, Celce-Murcia et al. (2010), Lane (2010), and Rogerson-Revell (2011) describe many options for teaching vowels and consonants in meaningful ways. The reason to work with vowel sounds is the enormous impact they have on broader features of pronunciation. Vowel sounds serve as the acoustic peaks of primary stressed syllables, which serve as the peaks of prominent words, which, in turn, serve as the peaks of thought groups. Collectively, these four elements represent the navigational guides listeners depend on to understand a speaker's meaning (Gilbert, 2009). Like the successive layers of an onion, vowels are closest to the core and each of the outer layers depends on their phonological integrity. When working with a core language sample, students' new task is to identify the particular vowel sounds that correspond with the primary stressed syllables of prominent words. For example, in thought groups . . .

// in b**a**ck of me // I heard a n**oi**se //

. . . they would learn to identify that the peak vowels of *b**a**ck* and *n**oi**se* rhyme with the vowels of *h**a**t* and *b**oy***, respectively. Clearly, teachers will need to be available to support learners' efforts for productive work with vowel sounds to happen. Eventually, students' rehearsal tasks can begin to incorporate their clearest enunciations possible of the peak vowels of prominent syllables. As mentioned earlier, and if it is relevant to learners' needs, audio recordings of at least one of their rehearsals is useful. Later, students can collaborate while analyzing recordings of their own performances for prominence and accuracy of vowel production.

Consonant Sounds

Much of what I just mentioned about the need for students to learn and work with vowel sounds is also applicable to the consonant sounds of English. Though consonants may not be as central as peak vowels to the rhythm system of English, Zielinski (2007) documents that non-native English speakers' levels of intelligibility improve as accuracy in the pronunciation of consonants located within primary stressed syllables (specifically) increases. In this sense, not all consonant locations merit equal attention. The consonants of stressed syllables matter more. A further implication of Zielinski's findings is that although consonants appearing within primary stressed syllables merit special attention, those appearing within prominent words are the most important of all. This is precisely where we can focus learners' attention with respect to consonant sounds. Also, a pervasive complication for many nonnative English speakers is a tendency to leave off final consonants. Consonants in word-final position also merit attention because English is permeated by the placement of grammatical markers at the ends of words (e.g., past tense, third person, suffixes, plural forms).

Body Language

> ### REFLECTIVE BREAK
>
> * What are some implications for pronunciation teaching in the following paraphrase?
>
>   *Communication in English is really a dance of the whole body. It's as if the sounds we make while speaking serve as music accompanying the rest of the communication. When we talk, the patterns of our speech flow in confluence with the motions of our hands and torso, the steps we take with our feet, the subtle ways in which we widen and narrow our eyes in connection with what we are saying. Sometimes it seems as if our whole bodies are in synchrony with the patterns of our speech.* (paraphrased from Wylie, 1985)

Once students have worked closely with a single core language sample over multiple days of class, another recommendation is to integrate connections between general speaking fluency, rhythmic features of pronunciation, and body language. Sometimes called "speech synchronized gestures" (e.g., hand gestures, head nods, walking in rhythm), students can learn to use them while rehearsing language samples (Acton, 2001, p. 203).

Before weaving body language into the teaching of pronunciation, however, we need to decide whether the topic is appropriate for the group. Some considerations are the maturity level and seriousness of purpose of the class, students' preferred learning styles, as well as any possible cultural impediments. If the decision is to go forward with attention to body language, we then need to decide which forms of speech synchronized gestures can and cannot be used with the groups (see the following list). A way to begin is to display a video of one or more English speakers who use hand gestures effectively. Following discussion of what students notice, an easy starting point is to teach students how to coordinate and time their use of simple hand gestures (e.g., tapping on desktops, pointing emphatically with index fingers) with their rehearsals of the primary stressed syllables of prominent words. Later, such activities can expand beyond practice with prominent words in isolation through rehearsals with the core language sample. By working with the full sample, the idea is to provide opportunities for learners to begin feeling the rhythm of spoken English. The teaching objective is for students to bring physical gestures into synchrony with the rhythm of the language sample they are rehearsing. Here are some examples of speech synchronized gestures worth introducing:

- lightly tapping pencils on desktops in synchrony with prominence and rhythm
- opening and closing hands (like clam shells) in similar ways
- walking around the room while coordinating footsteps with the primary stressed syllables of prominent words
- sharing handshakes and high fives so that partners' hands make momentary contact on the primary stressed syllable of prominent words
- alternately stretching thick rubber bands apart and relaxing them in synchrony with the stress patterns of prominent words
- taking easy dance steps coordinated with speech rhythms
- doing simple shoulder shrugs and/or raising eyebrows to indicate stressed syllables of prominent words
- playing hand games like "Pat-a-cake, Pat-a-cake" to illustrate rhythm

- while using nonthreatening boxing moves, gently sparring with partners to coordinate simulated jabs with stressed syllables of prominent words

Reflective Break

- Of the bulleted items listed above, which ones might be feasible to use in your classes?

- In what ways might some of them be problematic?

Conclusion

This book promotes a particular trajectory for teaching pronunciation in ESL/EFL classroom settings. Its starting point is the process of thought grouping (Chapter 1), to which successive layers of the architecture of English pronunciation are then added in manageable increments. After the foundational role that thought groups play has been established, students begin to work through a sequence of eight additional features of English pronunciation, each feature building upon those that came before. This particular instructional sequence engages learners in a process of working with prominence and featured words (Chapter 3); syllables, patterns of word stress, and primary stressed syllables (Chapter 4); as well as peak vowels, consonants, and body language (Chapter 5). Beginning with thought groups and continuing throughout the entire sequence, students work in teams as they apply what they are learning to their collaborative analysis and rehearsals (aloud) of a shared language sample. As discussed in Chapter 2, teachers select language samples to best suit learners' needs. After student teams have completed working through the full instructional sequence once, teachers introduce a new language sample, and the cycle repeats.

As learners gain more experience, teachers should explore ways of modifying and personalizing the ways of teaching and learning pronunciation that this book presents. When the time is right, a teacher might give students the opportunity to self-select pronunciation features with which they would like to spend more time, as well as those

that might merit less of their attention. Such decisions can be nego-
tiated between teacher and students as one way of keeping learner
motivation high. With teacher guidance and support, students can also
begin to self-select and find language samples they would prefer to
work with. Finally, it is worth keeping in mind that when it comes to
pronunciation learning, teachers can provide the most relevant information and best tools available, but ultimately learners' efforts are
what really matter most.

References

Acton, W. (2001). FocalSpeak: Integrating rhythm and stress in speech-pronunciation. In J. Murphy & P. Byrd (Eds.), *Understanding the courses we teach: Local perspectives on English language teaching* (pp. 197–217). Ann Arbor: University of Michigan Press.

Brazil, D. (1994). *Pronunciation for advanced learners of English.* New York, NY: Cambridge University Press.

Cauldwell, R. (2002). The functional irrhythmicality of spontaneous speech: A discourse view of speech rhythms. *Apples: Journal of Applied Language Studies, 2,* 1–24.

Celce-Murcia, M., Brinton, D., Goodwin, J., & Griner, B. (2010). *Teaching pronunciation: A course book and reference guide* (2nd ed.). New York, NY: Cambridge University Press.

Dauer, R. (1993). *Accurate English: A complete course in pronunciation.* Engle-wood Cliffs, NJ: Regents Prentice Hall.

Dickerson, W. (2010). Walking the walk: Integrating the story of English phonology. In J. M. Levis & K. LeVelle (Eds.), *Proceedings of the 1st pronunciation in second language learning and teaching conference* (pp. 10–23). Ames: Iowa State University.

Field, J. (2005). Intelligibility and the listener: The role of lexical stress. *TESOL Quarterly, 39,* 399–423. doi:10.2307/3588487

Gilbert, J. (2009). *Teaching pronunciation using the prosody pyramid.* New York, NY: Cambridge University Press.

Goodwin, J. (2001). Teaching pronunciation. In M. Celce-Murcia, D. M. Brinton, & M. A. Snow (Eds.), *Teaching English as a second or foreign language* (3rd ed., pp. 117–137). Boston, MA: Heinle Cengage.

Goodwin, J. (2014). Teaching pronunciation. In M. Celce-Murcia, D. M. Brinton, & M. A. Snow (Eds.), *Teaching English as a second or foreign language* (4th ed., pp. 136–152). Boston, MA: Heinle Cengage.

Grant, L. (2007). *Well said intro: Pronunciation for clear communication.* Boston, MA: Thomson/Heinle & Heinle.

Hahn, L. (2004). Primary stress and intelligibility: Research to motivate the teaching of suprasegmentals, *TESOL Quarterly, 38,* 201–223. doi:10.2307/3588378

Lane, L. (2010). *Tips for teaching pronunciation: A practical approach.* White Plains, NY: Pearson/Longman.

Morley, J. (1994). A multidimensional curriculum design for speech-pronunciation interaction. In J. Morley (Ed.), *Pronunciation pedagogy and theory: New views, new directions* (pp. 64–91). Alexandria, VA: TESOL.

Murphy, J. M. (2004). Attending to word-stress while learning new vocabulary. *English for Specific Purposes, 23,* 67–83. doi:10.1016/S0889-4906(03)00019-X

Rogerson-Revell, P. (2011). *English phonology and pronunciation teaching.* London, England: Continuum.

Wylie, L. (1985). Language learning and communication. *French Review, 58,* 777–785.

Zielinski, B. (2007). The listener: No longer the silent partner in reduced intelligibility. *System, 36,* 69–84. doi:10.1016/j.system.2007.11.004

Appendix

Answer Key for the
Airplane Aisle Incident Activity

For more advanced work: (1) draw a circle around any featured words within each thought group; (2) underline the single word within each thought group that would be the most prominent. The first three items have been completed for you (featured words in bold print; prominent words are also underlined).

Thought Groups (featured words indicated in bold)	Likely Number of Featured Words
//the plane **land**ed //	1 (*landed* is prominent)
//the **cabin** lights turned **on**//	2 (*cabin* is prominent; *on* is featured)
//**every**one got out of their **seats**//	2 (though either *everyone* or *seats* could be made prominent)[4]
//I **stepped** into the **aisle**//	2
//**opened** the overhead **compartment**//	2 (possibly 3)
//and was **waiting** my turn to **leave** the **plane**//	3 (possibly 2)
//in **back** of me//	1

---

[4]Variation is possible because the system of prominence is flexible and depends on the speaker's communicative intent.

Thought Groups (featured words indicated in bold)	Likely Number of Featured Words
//I heard a **noise** that **didn't** sound **right**//	3 (possibly 4)
//when I **turned**//	1
//I saw an **older** man//	1 (possibly 2)
//was **falling** into a woman **behind** him//	2 (possibly 3)
//he looked **scared**//	1
//his **face** was **stone white**//	3 (possibly 2)
//**I** didn't think he was **breathing**//	2
//I **yelled** for **help**//	2
//and then a **couple** of us moved into **action**//	2 (possibly 3)
//the **first** thing I did//	1
//was to get the people **behind** me to back **away**//	2 (possibly 3)
//by **this** point most of the **aisle** had **cleared**//	3
//so we were able to **stretch** him out on the **floor**//	2
//I **heard** someone **say**//	2 (possibly 1)
//we **have** to get him **out** of the plane//	2 (possibly 3)
//so I **grabbed** his **legs**//	2 (possibly 1)
//this **tall** guy grabbed his **shoulders**//	2 (possibly 3)
//and we **carried** him **off**//	2 (possibly 1)
//**I** know **CPR**//	4 (if it's // C // P // R //)
//so I **cleared** a space//	1 (possibly 2)
//made sure **everyone** else was **out** of the **way**//	3 (possibly 4)
//**fortunately**//	1 (which syllable?)
//when it was all **over**//	1 (possibly 2)
//he fully **recovered**//	1 (possibly 2)
//**seemed** to be **fine**//	2 (possibly 1)

Also Available in the English Language Teacher Development Series

Reflective Teaching (Thomas S. C. Farrell)

Teaching Listening (Ekaterina Nemtchinova)

Teaching Pronunciation (John Murphy)

Language Classroom Assessment (Liying Cheng)

Cooperative Learning and Teaching (George Jacobs & Harumi Kimura)

Classroom Research for Language Teachers (Tim Stewart)

Teaching Digital Literacies (Joel Bloch)

Teaching Reading (Richard Day)

Teaching Grammar (William Crawford)

Teaching Vocabulary (Michael Lessard-Clouston)

Teaching Writing (Zuzana Tomas, Ilka Kostka, & Jennifer A. Mott-Smith)

English Language Teachers as Administrators (Dan Tannacito)

Content-Based Instruction (Margo Dellicarpini & Orlando Alonso)

Teaching English as an International Language
(Ali Fuad Selvi & Bedrettin Yazan)

Teaching Speaking (Tasha Bleistein, Melissa K. Smith, & Marilyn Lewis)

tesol
international
association

www.tesol.org/bookstore
tesolpubs@brightkey.net
Request a copy for review
Request a Distributor Policy